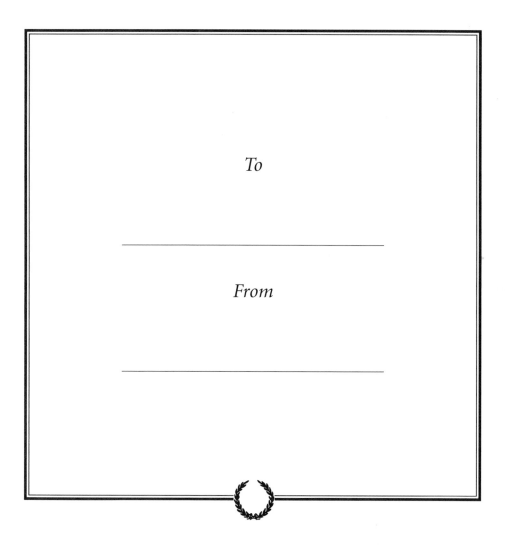

To

_____

From

_____

A Hero
In Every Heart

*Champions from all walks of life
share powerful messages
to inspire the hero
in each of us*

by H. Jackson Brown Jr. and Robyn Spizman

THOMAS NELSON PUBLISHERS
Nashville • Atlanta • London • Vancouver

Published in Nashville, Tennessee, by Thomas Nelson, Inc., and distributed in Canada by
Word Communications, Ltd., Richmond, British Columbia, and in the United Kingdom by
Word (UK), Ltd., Milton Keynes, England.

Scripture quotations are from the NEW KING JAMES VERSION of the Bible. Copyright ©
1979, 1980, 1982, 1990, 1994, Thomas Nelson, Inc., Publishers.

Material credited to HJB is original material from H. Jackson Brown Jr.

Material credited to Captain Scott O'Grady is taken from *Return with Honor* (New York:
Doubleday,1995).

Library of Congress-in-Publication Data

A hero in every heart : champions from all walks of life share powerful messages to inspire
the hero in each of us / [compiled] by H. Jackson Brown, Jr. and Robyn Spizman.
 p. cm.
 ISBN 0-7852-7349-2 CB
 1. Conduct of life—Quotations, maxims, etc. 2. Conduct of life—Literary collections.
I. Brown, H. Jackson, 1940- . II. Spizman, Robyn Freedman.
PN6084.C556H47 1996
082—dc20   96-7751
                                                                                              CIP

Printed in the United States of America
1 2 3 4 5 6 7 - 02 01 00 99 98 97 96

To Rosemary and Adam
–my heroes and my treasures.

—H. Jackson Brown Jr.

To the heroes in my life
and in my heart:
Willy, Justin, Ali, Mom, and Dad.
With love always.

—Robyn Spizman

Acknowledgments

Our sincere thanks go to the following individuals who fielded our calls, coordinated interviews, and championed our cause. Thanks to them, the inspiring words of great athletic champions are recorded in this book, as well as in our hearts:

Hillary Abbott, Andrew Adler, Kelly Baldwin, Rick Barney, Dan O'Brien, Helen Broder, Larry and Patty Brown, Pete Cava, Deedee Chereton, Paul Connell, Carol and Meredith DeChant, Jo Roberson Edwards, Jack and Phyllis Freedman, Doug and Genie Freedman, Brian Goldberg, Steve Graham, Glen Greenspan, Mike Gruber, Gail Heyman, Phil Isaacs, Michelle Jackson, Carolyn Koch, Pearce "Rocky" Lane, Brenda Laird, Mel Lehrner, Sandra Levy, Wayne Minshew, Marilyn J. Mitchell, Bruce and JacLynn Morris, John Morris, Phil Mulkey, Beverly Puckett, Jerry Rachelson, George Randazzo, Marla Shavin, Nica Shaw, Chuck Schupp, Bettye Storne, Craig Taubman, Nancy Trent, Sherry Villanueva, Michael Weinstock, Randy Waters, Chuck Watson, Ava Wilensky.

We would also like to thank Byron Williamson and Rolf Zettersten at Thomas Nelson Publishers, and Bruce Nygren for his wise counsel and fine editing.

$\mathcal{I}$ntroduction

ONCE IN A WHILE a person touches our lives with words and actions so special that they change us forever. These are the people who extend our vision and inspire us to higher levels of personal achievement. They are our heroes.

You'll find them in schoolrooms and locker rooms, on the assembly line and at the finish line, in foreign lands and right next door. You'll find them wherever the quest for personal excellence is practiced and wherever commitment to noble values is revered.

For centuries we've used the exemplary lives of heroes to teach us the benefits of persistence and commitment. And with today's creeping cynicsm and irreverence, the model of the hero becomes more important than ever. Heroes personify the best of what we want to believe about ourselves and offer proof that our grandest goals are achievable.

There is something in our spirit that longs to be elevated to new heights of purpose. Extraordinary achievements never fail to inspire us to raise our own sights and to color outside the lines. The celebration of heroes, we discover, is ultimately the celebration of our own potential.

We hope you find the stories and observations in this book inspiring lessons in the heroic qualities of sacrifice and virtue. And may you remember that regardless of where you find yourself on your life's journey, you never travel alone. For there, in your own heart, is a hero of epic proportion, ready at a moment's notice to join you in the grand struggle to seek and claim the ultimate prize—the satisfaction of a life of purpose, pursued with courage and passion.

H. J. B.
Tall Pine Lodge
Fernvale, Tennessee

*N*obody who
ever gave his best
regretted it.

—**George Halas**

A winner never stops trying.

—**TOM LANDRY**

I never blame fortune—there are too many complicated situations in life. But, I am absolutely merciless toward lack of effort.

—**F. SCOTT FITZGERALD**

*L*et your performance do the talking.

—**HJB**

*K*eep away from people who try to belittle your ambitions. Small people always do that, but the really great make you feel that you, too, can become great.

—**MARK TWAIN**

Here's a reminder that no one has yet found a way to get something for nothing. All worthwhile goals come at a price, and the coins with which we pay are concentration, persistence, and desire.

One of my favorite sayings I got off a soda bottle: NO DEPOSIT, NO RETURN. To me that means you'll get out of life about what you're willing to put in. All champions have made great sacrifices to win their victories. So when someone talks to me about their goals and dreams, I ask them one question: "What are you willing to do about it?"

—JOHN NABER
Four-time Olympic gold medalist, Swimming

*C*ourage is not defined by those
who fought and did not fall, but
by those who fought, fell,
and rose again.

Max Cleland inspires and challenges the hero in our hearts with this message of courage and commitment.

Whenever I've fallen, people I care about have been there to help me up. I feel so passionately that you never stand so tall as when you reach out to help another.

I believed in the idea of the self-made man until that grenade went off. I was laying on the battlefield without limbs. I had lost 40 percent of my body. Others came and saved my life. I see life differently now.

You can bounce back. It is possible to become strong in the broken places. You are a lot more courageous and heroic than you may think. Someone once said, "Adversity introduces a man to

*himself." For some that's scary, but most people
discover that adversity does make them stronger.
I got stronger. You have to in order to survive.*

—**MAX CLELAND**
*Secretary of state, Georgia
Head of Veterans Affairs under
President Jimmy Carter*

A hero is no braver than an ordinary
man, but he is braver five minutes
longer.

—**RALPH WALDO EMERSON**

Life doesn't
require that we
be the best, only that
we try our best.

—HJB

The more worthy the opponent, the better choice we have of performing at our best. And should we lose, we need to remember that the real benefit is not in the victory, but in the attempt.

Victory with honor and integrity is the real goal of sport. Sometimes it happens that others are better than you. I could never beat Carl Lewis in a hundred-yard dash, but my victory might be in running faster today than I did yesterday.

—DON SPARKS
Coach and athletic director

Winners in life are motivated to give more than is required and to do it with a cheerful spirit.

All through my professional and amateur career, I worked a little harder and trained a little extra. I was the first one at practice and the last one to leave. My philosophy was: Do what you're required to do, and then do a little more.

Because of my athletic accomplishments, I have the opportunity to speak to young people who may or may not be on the right path in life. I tell them that they can only reach their full potential by making the right choices, and I remind them that the right choices are seldom easy ones.

—**SAMUEL GRADY**
*Olympic gold medalist,
Track & Field*

*H*old yourself responsible to a higher standard than anyone else expects of you. Never excuse yourself.

—HENRY WARD BEECHER

*S*uccess seems to be largely a matter of hanging on after others have let go.

—WILLIAM FEATHER

*P*ursue perfection but accept excellence.

—HJB

Whatever we learn to do, we learn by actually doing it: men come to be builders, for instance, by building, and harp players by playing the harp. In the same way, by doing just acts, we come to be just; by doing self-controlled acts, we come to be self-controlled; and by doing brave acts, we become brave.

—ARISTOTLE

The friendships that develop when playing team sports often last a lifetime and are one of sports' greatest legacies.

Even when you've played the game of your life, it's the feeling of teamwork that you'll remember. You'll forget the plays, the shots, and the scores, but you'll never forget your teammates.

There are no free throws in life, even when you get fouled.

—DEBORAH MILLER PALMORE
Olympian, Basketball

*T*he will to win is important, but the will to prepare is vital.

—COACH JOE PATERNO

13

*N*o victory is
worth the sacrifice
of ideals.

—HJB

*T*he height of great men reached and
kept were not attained by sudden flight,
but they, while their companions slept,
were toiling upward in the night.

—**HENRY WADSWORTH LONGFELLOW**

*G*reat opportunities come to all, but
many do not know they have met them.
The only preparation to take advantage
of them is simple fidelity to what each
day brings.

—**A. W. DUNNING**

Great success demands great sacrifice—usually by many people.

Most people don't realize how many people it takes for one person to succeed and the sacrifices that have to be made. Without the encouragement of my parents and my husband, I would have quit. My parents took me to meets which were expensive. My husband knew how tired I'd be when I got home from work, so he made dinner. I never would have won a gold medal without my family—they're the ones who made the sacrifices. I'm the one who gets all the glory. I wasn't the only one who won that medal. My family deserves it too.

Although not everyone's going to win a gold medal at the Olympics, everyone can set personal goals. Striving to reach the goals is an achievement in itself. Satisfaction comes from knowing you've given it your best shot. When you've done everything you know how to do and don't make it, you can still feel successful. Then you'll never have to look back and say, "If I had only tried." Who wants to live life remembering and regretting a lot of "What ifs"?

—ANGEL MYERS MARTINO
Olympic gold medalist,
Swimming

$\mathcal{F}$ame is fleeting.
Money takes wing.
Popularity is an accident.
The only thing that remains is character.

*Y*our mind can only hold one thought at a time—make it a positive and constructive one.

—**HJB**

*W*hat matters is not the size of the dog in the fight, but the size of the fight in the dog.

—**Coach Paul "Bear" Bryant**

*F*orget about style; worry about results.

—**Bobby Orr**

$\mathcal{I}$t doesn't
take talent to
hustle.

—HJB

*T*he marvelous richness of human experience would lose something of rewarding joy if there were no limitations to overcome. The hilltop hour would not be half so wonderful if there were no dark valleys to traverse.

—**HELEN KELLER**

*T*he quality of your life is determined by the quality of the people in your life.

—**HJB**

Ultimately we are remembered for what we give, not for what we take.

My favorite motto is: "Try to bring a rainbow to someone's life every day." What sort of legacy will we leave? What will they put on our tombstone? I want mine to read that I made a difference in somebody's life!

—GRACE KREMER
Masters, Archery

*N*othing is so potent as the silent influence of a good example.

—JAMES KENT

*M*ay our adversities make us strong.
May our victories make us wise.
May our actions make us proud.

—HJB

*G*ood character is that quality which makes one dependable whether being watched or not, which makes one truthful when it is to one's advantage to be a little less than truthful, which makes one courageous when faced with great obstacles, which endows one with the firmness of wise self-discipline.

—**ARTHUR S. ADAMS**

Winners are self-motivated. They don't wait for someone else to raise the bar. They raise it themselves.

Champions arrive early and stay late. They know what they're there for. They don't have to be told five times to do something or be given a five-minute lecture on how to do it. You give them the challenge, and they get it done.

There are people who work at 50 percent of their ability and who are successful. Then there are the ones who give 110 percent of everything they've got and barely make it. Which ones would you want? I'd rather have the people who give it their all and walk off the field knowing that. In business as in athletics, a champion is the person who at the end says, "I gave it everything I had; win or lose, you got the best I can give."

I was a baseball player until I got hurt. I got stabbed in the back; just a matter of being in the wrong place at the wrong time. People say that's too bad, but I say it's no big deal. That was yesterday. I went from being a baseball player to having the chance to do something all over again. How many people get a second chance? Had this not happened, I wouldn't be a paralympic athlete. I look it at this way: Life is more of a mental challenge than a physical one. Your arms and legs get you where you're going, but once you're there, it's your mind that's important.

—**JAMES WILLIAMS**
Paralympian, Table Tennis

Thoughts become actions; actions become habits; habits become character; character becomes destiny.

I believe in practicing like a champion. When it was just a training session early in the season, I tried to create in my mind the World Cup or Olympic Games, and I practiced as if I was actually there. If you practice like a champion, when you get to the big event, you're prepared.

You're not always going to win. In Lillehammer, I placed fourth, but I raced faster than I had ever skated in my entire life. To me, I was a winner. I was happy with my performance because I had accomplished something I had never done before.

—**BONNIE BLAIR**
*Olympic gold medalist,
Speed Skating*

*E*xcellence is
immortal.

—HJB

*F*ate often saves a warrior when his courage endures.

—**BEOWOLF**

*W*hatever your hand finds to do, do it with your might.

—**ECCLESIASTES 9:10**

*F*ight your fears with action.

—**HJB**

*T*he credit belongs to those who are actually in the arena, who strive valiantly; who know the great enthusiasm, the great devotions, and spend themselves in a worthy cause; who at the best, know the triumph of high achievement; and who, at the worst, if they fail, fail while daring greatly, so that their place shall never be with those cold and timid souls who know neither victory nor defeat.

—THEODORE ROOSEVELT

A great attitude always precedes a great performance.

A champion is someone who has an outlook of optimism. It's an attitude: the ability to see the opportunity in the problem.

Persistence is also important because no one accomplishes everything on the first try. Some people believe in beginner's luck. But luck eventually runs out, and then it's just you and your commitment.

Pil Sung is a Korean word I learned when I took Choi Kwang Do. It means "indomitable spirit." It reminds me that you can't let your spirit get down because your body will follow.

—**JARED HEYMAN**
High school student, wrestler, Eagle Scout

$\mathcal{Y}$ou can't stuff
a great life
into a small dream.

—HJB

We first make our habits, then our habits make us. Habits, good or bad, begin as innocent companions. Later they become our masters.

Along the way I acquired the habit of not compromising. I learned that you do what you say you were going to do. It's easy to put together a plan and state goals at the beginning, but when you're three or four months into a heavy training schedule, it's more difficult to accomplish everything on your list. I learned not to leave the gym until I did everything I said I was going to do.

I tell young athletes to practice as if it were competition, but compete as if it were practice. Everybody works hard when they feel like it, but only the best do it when they don't feel like it.

We all are originals. Even faced with terrible peer pressure, you need to be your own person.

❧

I was the only gymnast in my school. I could have said, "Peter, no one does gymnastics. It's not hip." That's the problem with kids who get involved with drugs. They don't have the courage to say, "I'm not going to follow that crowd." But it's even more hip and more cool to be true to yourself, even at the risk of ridicule by those who call you their friend.

—**PETER VIDMAR**
Two-time Olympic gold medalist, Gymnastics

*P*eople who accomplish big things did small things well.

—**HJB**

*T*he minute you start talking about what you're going to do if you lose, you have lost.

—**George Schultz**

*E*very great and commanding movement in the annals of the world is the triumph of enthusiasm. Nothing great was ever achieved without it.

—**Ralph Waldo Emerson**

*N*o champion is embarrassed by his scars.

—**HJB**

We are always surprised
at the progress that
comes from doing
simple things well.

—HJB

Every contest is a new opportunity to test our courage and renew our commitment.

There is a sign in the Notre Dame locker room above the door that leads onto the field. It was a tradition that when the team would go through the door, each of us would touch it. It reads: Play like a champion.

To me that meant to go out and play your best. Even if things don't go the way you want, if you've done your best, you can feel good about it.

—CHRISTOPHER ZORICH
Chicago Bears Lineman
All-Time All-American
at Notre Dame

*T*he best preparation for tomorrow is doing your best today.

—HJB

*E*xcellence is never an accident; it is always the result of high intention, determined effort, and skilled execution.

*T*he gem cannot be polished without friction, nor man perfected without trials.

—Chinese proverb

*G*ood, Better, Best.
Never rest
Until good be better
And better best.

—**MOTHER GOOSE**

*B*y every part of our nature we clasp
things above us, one after another, not
for the sake of remaining where we take
hold, but that we may go higher.

—**H. W. BEECHER**

Faith has
won many
a race.

Success doesn't discriminate. It's an equal opportunity employer—available to everyone willing to pay the price.

It's amazing where hard work can take you. One year I came out of nowhere to win the world championship. That's the way it is in life. You can rise above almost any obstacle if you're willing to work hard and believe that you can do it. I want everyone to remember that ordinary people can do extraordinary things.

—Dr. Thad Bell
Assistant Dean
University of South Carolina
Medical School
(World's Fastest Human
over Age 40, 1987)

*T*alent without discipline is like an octopus on roller skates. There's plenty of movement, but you never know if it's going to be forward, backwards, or sideways.

—HJB

*C*ompeting in sports has taught me that if I'm not willing to give 120 percent, somebody else will.

—RON BLOMBERG
Former New York Yankee

*T*hose who strive to be above average soon are.

—HJB

When you get into a tight place and everything goes against you, till it seems as though you could not hold on a minute longer, never give up then, for that is just the place and time that the tide will turn.

—**HARRIET BEECHER STOWE**

Opportunity dances with those who are already on the dance floor.

—**HJB**

We are not born brave and heroic. It's the result of a decision we make when we choose to live lives based on noble principles inspired by courage and impelled by commitment.

I have RP, a genetic disease that causes you to slowly lose your vision, like a slow leak in a tire. Thirteen years after I was diagnosed, my lights went out.

Today, I'm a raging bull. I haven't even made a dent yet. I took all my negative energy and focused it on doing positive things. I don't want to be remembered as a person who set world records for the blind; I want to be remembered as a person who helped others.

Disability is only a state of mind. In my opinion the human body is a container, and the container comes in different sizes and shapes and colors. Some have no hair; some are long and slender or short and stout. Some have no headlights like me.

The important thing to remember is that the essence of our humanity is the spirit that lies within our container. We all have this spirit, and it is a reservoir of tremendous potential. When you tap into this potential, you can move mountains. And if you can't do that, you can still drill right through them.

—RICH RUFFALO
Paralympic gold medalist, Discus
Outstanding Teacher of the Year in 1995
Outstanding Coach of the Year in 1995
National Teacher's Hall of Fame

$\mathcal{T}$hose who turn
back never reach
the summit.

—HJB

*N*ever esteem anything as of advantage
to thee that shall make thee break thy
word or lose thy self-respect.

—**MARCUS AURELIUS**

*P*eople never improve unless they look
to some standard or example higher or
better than themselves.

—**TYRONE EDWARDS**

*W*inners are like biscuits—when things
heat up, they rise to the occasion.

—**HJB**

It's easier to establish and pursue goals when we know what our priorities are.

A friend who was a great influence on me was a war hero in the first world war. He was an Italian commander who became a successful businessman. He said you should live every day to the fullest, and your family should be your focus in life. That was the extent of his philosophy, and to me it was enough.

—ROBERTO ALVA
Olympian, Fencing

*B*etter be three hours too soon than one minute too late.

—SHAKESPEARE

When your opponent is
bigger, faster, stronger,
train harder, longer,
smarter.

—HJB

THE BOOMERANG THEORY:
When you give your best to the world,
the world returns the favor.

—**HJB**

No man who is occupied in doing a
very difficult thing, and doing it very
well, ever loses his self-respect.

—**GEORGE BERNARD SHAW**

*N*othing in the world can take the place of persistence.

Talent will not; nothing is more common than unsuccessful men with talent.

Genius will not; unrewarded genius is almost a proverb.

Education will not; the world is full of educated derelicts.

Persistence and determination alone are omnipotent.

—CALVIN COOLIDGE

Winners come in all shapes and sizes, but they all have one thing in common—a big heart.

People say to me, "You're so short" or "You're so young." I just say to them, "That just gives me more years to beat you!" My mother always told me, "Dynamite comes in small packages."

—**MELISSA PRICE**
Pioneer in women's pole vault
American women's record holder

*N*othing can stop the man with the right mental attitude from achieving his goal; nothing on earth can help the man with the wrong mental attitude.

—**THOMAS JEFFERSON**

*I*n every child who is born, under no matter what circumstances, and of no matter what parents, the potentiality of the human race is born again: and in him, too, once more, and of each of us, our terrific responsibility toward human life; toward the utmost ideals of goodness, of the horror of terror, and of God.

—**JAMES AGEE**

Here is a sure formula for success: Outwork the competition.

Some days, when I didn't feel like working out, I'd think about the guys I would compete against, and I'd realize that they were probably working out. That's all it took to keep me going.

An old man gave me some advice very early in my track-and-field career. His name was Bill Foster, and he was at that time a baseball pitcher with the Indianapolis Clowns. It was 1958, and he said, "You look like you're going to be a pretty good athlete. Let me tell you something. You meet the same people twice in life—on your way up and on your way back down. Their treatment of you the second time depends entirely on how you treat them the first time."

Years ago I cut something out of a golf magazine. It was about Sam Snead, and I carried it in my billfold until it fell apart. It told about this guy who played a round with Sam. On the first hole, Sam made a seven—three strokes over par. As they exited the green to go to the next hole, Sam was unruffled. "That's why we play eighteen holes," he said. His round ended that day four under par. To me that says keep your cool and don't give up.

Being the first to cross the finish line makes you a winner in only one phase of life. It's what you do after you cross the line that really counts.

—RALPH BOSTON
*Olympic gold medalist,
Track & Field*

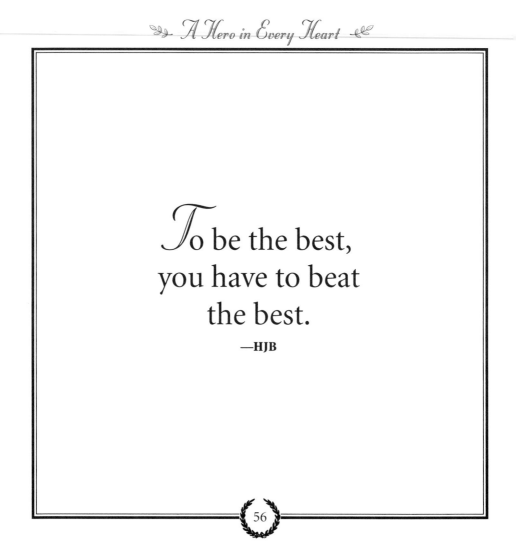

To be the best,
you have to beat
the best.

—HJB

*T*he opportunity to do better tomorrow than you did today is a privilege—and a duty.

*T*he greatest test of courage on earth is to bear defeat without losing heart.

—**ROBERT GREEN INGERSOLL**

*I*ndividuals play the game, but teams win championships.

—**SIGN IN NEW ENGLAND PATRIOTS' LOCKER ROOM**

Victory comes at a price. The question we must ask ourselves is: "What are we willing to pay?"

While I was competing I said to myself, "How bad do you want it?" I used that logic and that phrase whenever I trained and competed. Did I really want it more than the other person?

—**Sharon Jewell**
Olympic bronze medalist,
Tae Kwon Do

I'm going to do it or die trying.

—**Almost everyone at one time in their life**

You can't
hire someone to
practice for you.

—HJB

With a positive attitude and encouragement from coaches, family, and friends, there's no limit to what we can do.

I had taken my sight for granted. Stop and look around; it can happen to anyone. No one is immune to any hardship—physical, mental, or emotional. Mine is physical, but we all need to respect each other no matter what challenge we face.

Determination is the key factor. If every time life threw you a curve, you gave up, you'd never go forward. Staying in the game requires a mental toughness, and with that attitude anything is possible.

—**JENNIFER ARMBRUSTER**
Paralympian, Goalball

*W*hen you win, nothing hurts.

—JOE NAMATH

*L*ife's battles don't always go
To the stronger or faster man;
But soon or late, the man who wins
Is the one who thinks he can.

—C. W. LONGENECKER

*T*he biggest gap in the world is between
"I should" and "I did."

—HJB

Winners don't dwell on past mistakes. They learn from the experiences and move on with new spirit and resolve.

A real winner is someone who can win the game at the buzzer, score the touchdown in the final seconds, and hit a home run when you're down by one in the bottom of the ninth.

The people who close out the game are so rare and so special that when they come along, we practically turn them into athletic gods.

Magic Johnson, Michael Jordan, Joe Montana, Kareem Abdul Jabar, Larry Bird, Wayne Gretsky—these are the winners or "closers" who taught me a great lesson: When you make a mistake or miss a shot, you don't fix it the next day or the next week. You fix it that moment by being able to move on.

They can make a mistake and not let it ruin the whole game for them.

Michael can miss seven shots in a row and not hesitate a moment to shoot the eighth. He says to himself, "I know I'm not terrible. I just have to keep shooting until I hit one."

The thing to learn from winners is how to move on. Great athletes have incredible capacity to forget their mistakes. So, learn from your mistakes, but don't dwell on them.

—PAT O'BRIEN
CBS Sports host

*I*t's always too soon
to quit.

—DAVID TYLER SCOATES

What is defeat? Nothing but education; nothing but the first step to something better.

—**RICHARD SHERIDAN**

Great works are performed, not by strength, but by perseverance.

—**SAMUEL JOHNSON**

The greater the obstacle, the more glory in overcoming it.

—**MOLIERE**

Examples of true courage never fail to lift our spirits and warm our hearts.

My competitive spirit didn't stop because I became disabled physically. I never asked, "Why me?" After my car accident I still said, "Now, what's my purpose?"

The courage of a friend named Emery Lawrence motivated me. He was a double amputee and was on dialysis. I drove him to get treatment three times a week. Then he had a stroke and could only use one arm. He was thirty-nine when he passed away, and in my eyes he was a champion. He taught me this: Quitting is not an option.

—JOSEPH RUSSELL
Paralympian, Powerlifting

I love the man that can smile in trouble, that can gather strength from distress, and grow brave by reflection. 'Tis the business of little minds to shrink, but he whose heart is firm, and whose conscience approves his conduct, will pursue his principles unto death.

—**Thomas Paine**

*I*t is the last step in a race that counts.

It is the last stroke on the nail that counts.

Many a prize has been lost just when it was ready to be plucked.

—Anonymous

It takes so little effort to offer encouragement—a smile, a touch, a few well-spoken words.

I played pathetically in my first freshman game at Dartmouth, but for some reason the coach believed in me. He came to me after the game and said, "Don't worry, you'll do better. We're playing this game for fun." The next game, I played fabulously. After I graduated I played pro football. Isn't it amazing what a little encouragement can do!

I ask young athletes, "How do you train?" If you find glory in the process, then training and preparation will be an uplifting experience. Training prepares you for one of the greatest experiences in life—the discovery that you have exceeded your own expectations.

—REGGIE WILLIAMS
Former Cincinnati Bengals linebacker

Champions know there are no short-cuts to the top. They climb the mountain one step at a time. They have no use for helicopters!

—**Judi Adler**
Olympian, Figure Skating

Fortune favors the bold.

—**Virgil**

All champions share this one rule: to finish the task.

—**HJB**

*P*roper preparation
solves 80 percent
of life's problems.

—HJB

No one makes it to the top without a lot of assistance along the way. We should be quick and generous in acknowledging those who help us.

People think of swimming as an individual sport, but I never could have accomplished what I did without my teammates and the support of my family. It's a lot easier to achieve great things when you have the help of great people. When victory comes, they're part of it.

Swimming has been a significant part of my life. I've gotten so much from it—including my husband, Mark. I met him at the Olympics where he was swimming for the Australian team. He won two silver medals and a bronze in 1984. We live in Australia and are the proud parents of twins, William and Maddison.

I've discovered it's not whether you reach your goal that's most important, but what you learn on your journey. What I remember now as I look back on my swimming career is not the records or gold medals, but how the experiences and the wonderful people I met contributed to who I am today. I learned how to handle the ups and downs and the pressure. I use these lessons every day.

—**TRACY CAULKINS STOCKWELL**
Three-time Olympic gold medalist, Swimming

The Champion's Creed

1. Never underestimate your opponent.

2. Work on your weaknesses until they become your strong points.

3. Remember that a great effort is usually the result of a great attitude.

4. Dedicate yourself to a mighty purpose.

5. Win with humility, lose with grace.

6. Ignore those who discourage you.

7. Work to improve your moral and spiritual strengths as well as your physical ones.

8. Remember that how you conduct yourself off the field is just as important as how you conduct your self on the field.

9. Talent is God-given—be humble.
Fame is man-given—be thankful.
Conceit is self-given—be careful.

10. Don't ask to be deprived of tension and
discipline—these are the tools
that shape success.

11. Do what has to be done,
when it has to be done, and as well
as it can be done.

12. Remember that when you're not working
to improve, your competition is.

13. Always give your best.

14. Practice like a champion.

15. Play like a champion.

16. Live like a champion.

—HJB

*I*t wasn't the reward that mattered or the recognition you might harvest. It was your depth of commitment, your quality of service, the product of your devotion—these were the things that counted in a life. When you gave purely, the honor came in the giving, and that was honor enough.

—**Capt. Scott O'Grady**

A brave heart
is a powerful
weapon.

—HJB

Winners look for opportunities, and when they don't find any, make them.

When I was a young boy, I lived on a farm in the Ozark foothills of Missouri. We didn't even have electricity. We were very poor, but we didn't know it because everyone we knew was equally poor. The point is, my making the Olympic team was an incredible feat for me.

When I was fifteen, the great Olympian Bob Matthias was my inspiration. I thought if he could do it, I could do it. I ran all over the farm to build my endurance and practiced the high hurdles by jumping over barbed-wire fences. I knocked the iron head off a post mall to use as a shot put. I practiced throwing the discus by throwing a round plow shear. My javelin was a pitchfork handle minus the forks. People must have thought I was crazy. But I had a dream and was committed to doing the best with what I had. And my dream did come true. After trying for twelve years, I made the Olympic team in 1960.

I'm now over sixty years old and enjoy competing in the Masters Program. But Mother Nature is trying to take charge of my life. I can live with Mother Nature, but if she thinks her struggle with me is going to be an easy one, she's got another thing coming. After all, I'm the one who used to jump over barbed-wire fences.

—**PHIL MULKEY**
Olympian, Decathlon

*I*t's hard to beat a person who never gives up.

—**BABE RUTH**

*Y*ou gain strength, courage, and confidence by every experience in which you really stop to look fear in the face . . . you must do the thing you think you cannot do.

—**ELEANOR ROOSEVELT**

*I*f a man has a talent and cannot use it, he has failed. If he has a talent and uses only half of it, he has partly failed. If he has a talent and learns somehow to use the whole of it, he has gloriously succeeded and has a satisfaction and a triumph few men ever know.

—**THOMAS WOLFE**

$\mathcal{S}$uccess
stops when
you do.

—HJB

Practice doesn't make perfect. Perfect practice makes perfect.

Champions execute the fundamentals with unconscious competence. That means they've practiced the moves so many times in the past that they can do them almost perfectly without thinking about it. When you can perform brilliantly without thinking, you can perform at a very high level.

—**JUNE JONES**
Atlanta Falcons coach

An expert at anything was once a beginner.

—**HJB**

*T*he high sentiments always win in the end, the leaders who offer blood, toil, tears, and sweat always get more out of their followers than those who offer safety and a good time. When it comes to the pinch, human beings are heroic.

—**GEORGE ORWELL**

*T*here is only one real failure in life that is possible, and that is not to be true to the best we know.

—**FREDERICK FARRAR**

Whether you come in first or not, performing at your highest level makes you a winner.

At age eighty-three, I've had to adjust to the fact that I'm not as fast as I was at seventy-three or even sixty-three. Even if I don't win the medals, I get up and do my best, and I'm satisfied with my performance.

❧

You have to do the best you can under the circumstances and realize there's no point in getting upset. You'll run into difficulties, and if you can change or improve the situation, change it. If you can't, don't fret about it.

—Bob Boal
*Masters gold medalist,
Track & Field*

From an early age champions master the art of turning stumbling blocks into stepping stones. "No excuses, just results" becomes their philosophy.

I trained on dirt roads. If you have the desire, you won't let poor facilities, poor equipment, or anything keep you from reaching your goals. Determination is everything.

—**ALICE COACHMAN**
Olympic gold medalist,
Track & Field

*T*he worst bankruptcy in the world is the person who has lost his enthusiasm.

—**H. W. ARNOLD**

Most look up
and admire the stars.
A champion climbs
a mountain and
grabs one.

—HJB

Inside each of us are powers so strong, treasures so rich, possibilities so endless, that to command them all to action would change the history of the world.

When I was born with spina bifida, doctors thought I'd never walk and would be dependent on my parents for the rest of my life. But I showed them. I started to walk when I was two and used braces until I was a freshman in high school.

When I was a junior, I met another kid in a wheelchair. He told me that you could play soccer in a wheelchair. He kept trying to get me involved, and I finally decided to try out. It was competitive and not patronizing. We crashed and banged, and bodies flew. When we fell, we'd climb back in our chairs. I loved it.

After that I discovered football, basketball, square dancing, softball, tennis, racquetball, and waterskiing. I tried them all. There's so much you can do in a wheelchair.

Recently, I went jogging with the president. Each year President Clinton invites the winners of the Boston Marathon, including the wheelchair winner, to jog with him. He told me that I have the best-looking arms in America. In fact, when he gave me his autograph, he wrote, "To Jean, the best-looking arms in America."

Some people think that successful persons are born that way. I'm here to tell you that a champion is someone who has fallen off the horse a dozen times and gotten back on the horse a dozen times. Successful people never give up.

—JEAN DRISCOLL

Six-time Boston Marathon winner (Wheelchair Division) Paralympic gold medalist, Track & Field

Boast less.
Boost more.

—HJB

All of us like to practice the skills we do well. But winners discipline themselves to work on their weaknesses until they become their strengths.

The difference between a good athlete and a top athlete is that the top athlete will do the mundane things when nobody's looking. That's what separates champions from the others.

A champion is someone who pays attention to the little things, such as conditioning, proper nutrition, and diet. They do it to be a champion, not just because somebody told them to do it. Larry Bird, for example, was the first one to arrive at practice and the last one to leave. He was always working on some part of his game that he felt needed improving.

—**SUSAN TRUE**
*National Federation of State
High School Associations*

We are ultimately judged not by our triumphs but by how we conduct ourselves during the struggle. By being true to our convictions and always trying our best, we never disappoint others or ourselves.

When I was eleven years old, I skated my first national championship. I thought I was going to win, but I came in second. My dad supported and encouraged us, but he always kept things in perspective. As I was waiting for some great words of wisdom from him, he said, "There's more to life than skating around in a circle." This upset me because I thought he didn't have any idea how important this was to me. But in 1988, when my sister died of leukemia, I understood what he meant.

We need to be able to learn something from any situation. It's easy to take something good from a positive situation, but we also need to know how to learn from difficult times.

When people think of me, I would like to be remembered as someone who never gave up. I never lost hope, but more importantly, I skated my best, not only when I won the gold medal, but also those times when I fell or was beaten. Each time it was the same for me; it was the best I had to give.

—**DAN JANSEN**
Olympic gold medalist,
Speed Skating

*S*uccess isn't forever, and failure isn't fatal.

—**FAVORITE SAYING OF**
COACH DON SHULA

Dream big.
There is little power
in little plans.

—**HJB**

*I*t is not the size of a man but the size of his heart that matters.

—**EVANDER HOLYFIELD**
Three-time world champion,
Boxing

*T*he real contest is always between what you've done and what you're capable of doing. You measure yourself against yourself and nobody else.

—**GEOFFREY GABERINO**
Olympic gold medalist,
Swimming

Humility is the sign of maturity and a characteristic of a true champion.

No one is invincible, and at a given time, anyone can win. You need a balance between confidence and humility. Proper training, the right attitude, and the support of family and friends give you confidence. But you need humility too. It keeps you honest.

Defeat teaches you that the things which don't kill you make you stronger—both mentally and physically.

—Dr. Jonathan Davis
Boxing Cornerman/Cutman

My dad used to say, "A tree doesn't fall at the first stroke." When we commit ourselves to a task, we need to see it through to the end.

I've always been inspired by a quote from John D. Rockefeller:

> *I don't think there is any other quality so essential to success of any kind as the quality of perseverance. It overcomes almost everything, even nature.*

This quote stands out to me because when I was ready to throw in the towel, it was my perseverance that got me through it all. I reminded myself of that one word.

—**ANN CODY**
*Paralympic gold medalist,
Track & Field*

Life is sometimes kind enough to offer us a second chance.

In the 1984 Olympics I was a newcomer, but I had set the world record in the 100-meter butterfly and was considered the favorite. During the race a swimmer named Michael Gross came from behind and won by 15/100ths of a second.

In 1992 I decided to make a comeback. Most people thought that because I was twenty-seven and had been out of the water for three years, I had no chance of winning a gold medal. But I was excited about my goal, and I became better at motivating myself. When I woke up each morning at five, I would ask myself, "Why am I doing this?" I would then focus on my long-term and daily goals. More than natural ability, focusing throughout the day on these goals had a lot to do with my success.

I did fulfill my goal in 1992 and won the gold medal by 3/100ths of a second.

—**PABLO MORALES**
Olympic gold medalist,
100-Meter Butterfly

*N*ature cannot be tricked or cheated. She will give up to you the object of your struggles only after you have paid her price.

—**NAPOLEON HILL**

The Price

*Y*ou pay a price for getting stronger.

You pay a price for getting faster.

You pay a price for jumping higher.

You pay a price for staying just the same.

—HJB

Do you not know that those who run in a race all run, but one receives the prize? Run in such a way that you may obtain it.

—1 Corinthians 9:24

My message to you is:
Be courageous! . . . Be as brave as your fathers before you. Have faith! Go forward.

—Thomas A. Edison

When within your heart you have determined your life's mission, let not the mightiest army keep you from your goal.

I was born in a very modest, rural home filled with love, an absence of prejudice, and a clear understanding of right and wrong. As I traveled down life's highway, I might have sometimes swerved from one side of the road to the other, but because of the values my parents taught me, I never found myself in a ditch.

I knew from an early age that I wanted to be a coach. My sisters tried to talk me out of it. They said I'd never make any money. But I told them I had something better than money—a mission!

Working with young people, I meet a lot of parents. They love their children so much that they often spoil them by giving them everything they want and by not allowing them to suffer the consequences of their actions. But children should be accountable for their behavior. It's the best way for them to become caring and responsible adults. Many parents also think that constant bragging about their children builds their self-esteem. I've found that children best learn self-esteem by making the right decisions in tough situations and by completing difficult tasks.

In a way we are all coaches; someone younger and less experienced is always looking at us as an example of how they should conduct their life.

—RON BELL
National High School Basketball Coach of the Year

*I*f I do not practice one day, I know it. If I do not practice the next, the orchestra knows it. If I do not practice the third day, the whole world knows it.

—**IGNAC PADEREWSKI**

*W*isdom, compassion, and courage— these are the three universally recognized moral qualities of men.

—**CONFUCIUS**

There will always be people who will tell you that your dreams are too big, your hopes too unattainable. Ignore them.

I always wanted to run, swim, and play able-bodied sports, but they wouldn't let me in high school because they were worried I'd get hurt. But when somebody tells me I can't do something, I just say, "I can." I just keep going. I don't let negative people stop me. There's always somebody who is negative, and you can't let that bother you. You've got to keep on going.

The most important thing in my life is to continue setting goals. The gold medal was the end result for 1992, but when the plane landed back in America, I set my sights on 1996.

—**LARRY BANKS**
Paralympic gold medalist,
100-Meter Dash

*W*inners do
what losers don't
want to do.

—HJB

You play the way you practice.

When I jumped I would say to myself, "This is your day, and no one can beat you." I said that every time I competed, and I only lost once. And the one time I lost was because I hadn't trained like I should have. I decided if I was going to compete, I'd be ready.

Never get too comfortable; the time to relax is when the event is over.

—MILDRED MCDANIELS SINGLETON
Olympic gold medalist, High Jump

*I*t's not over till it's over.

—YOGI BERRA

Today is the day we've waited for all our lives.

My daddy gave me some great advice when I was seven years old. He said, "When your feet hit the floor every morning, say out loud, 'Today I'm going to do the best job I can do.'" Today is a promise you make to yourself.

—**PEARCE "ROCKY" LANE**
President, Georgia Olympians
World champion boxer

*L*uck marches with those who give their very best.

—**HJB**

*S*uccess is written in ice, and eventually the sun comes out.

—**Joe Garigiola**

*B*ravery never goes out of fashion.

—**William M. Thackeray**

*T*he view from the top is great, but don't miss the many scenic overlooks along the way.

—**HJB**

*N*othing important
was ever achieved without
someone taking
a chance.

—HJB

A team's true spirit and character are revealed not when they're winning, but when they're losing.

—HJB

*I*t is not ease but effort, not facility but difficulty, that makes man. There is perhaps no station in life in which difficulties do not have to be encountered and overcome before any decided means of success can be achieved.

—Samuel Smiles

Randy Snow's courage and indomitable spirit prove again that success in life is 10 percent what happens to us and 90 percent what we do about it.

In 1975 I was injured in a farming accident. I was introduced to wheelchair sports a few years later. It became a way for me to deal with my disability.

You compare able-bodied athletes to disabled athletes differently. The disabled athlete has to go through an acceptance process. You have to say, "Life has dealt me a bad hand; am I okay with missing part of my body?" Once you accept yourself and say, "This is who I am," you really go at it. It's like you owe life one. You want to get life back. You decide this isn't going to stop you. It's just going to make you tougher.

You can celebrate being a champion only until midnight. Because if you carry it any further, your competition is gaining ground. If you win the national championship that day, then you can enjoy it, but only until midnight. Then it's back to work.

—**RANDY SNOW**
Paralympic gold medalist,
Tennis

If you are doing your best, you will not have to worry about failure.

—**ROBERT HILLYER**

$\mathcal{S}$weat is
the lubricant
of success.

—HJB

"The watchword of life must be, never give up." Too often we quit when victory is only moments away. Success is ours when we hold on just one second longer than the competition.

Life teaches us about the law of averages. You can't get a hit in life if you don't keep on swinging. A quitter never wins and a winner never quits. There are people who whistle while they work and are magnificent at life, but then there are moaners and whiners. I tell kids, "Don't blame, complain, or explain."

The higher the level you play, the less they accept excuses.

—Lt. Col. McDonald Valentine
Professional baseball tutor and coach

Praise those who try. Console those who lose. Celebrate those who win.

Everyone who is talented doesn't always win. I tell my own son, "Mommy's not going to win all the time." Always put in the effort. That's the main thing.

—**GWENN TORRENCE**
olympic gold medalist,
200-meter

*E*xcellence is never granted to a man but as the reward of labor.

—**SIR JOSHUA REYNOLDS**

$\mathcal{S}$uccess is
like a garden;
it always needs
tending.

—HJB

Never give up on yourself or anyone else—miracles happen every day.

After two years of playing college basketball, my coach told me I was the worst player he'd ever coached and suggested I might have a better chance at volleyball. So two things happened: I made the U.S. National Volleyball Team, and I vowed that I'd never get cut from anything again.

I love to tell this story about the power of sports. The mayor of Miami called the heads of two rival gangs, a black gang and a Cuban gang, into his office. They'd been involved in beatings, drive-by shootings—really nasty stuff. The mayor said, "I want each of you to get a teammate from your club and play at Hoop It Up Miami."

The first game started, and the Cubans were on one side and the blacks were on the other side of the court—totally separated. But before the tournament was over, they were playing together as a team. They learned that they were much the same—they sweated, laughed, and struggled as teammates.

That's the power of sports: It has a way of bringing people from different backgrounds closer together.

—**TERRY MURPHY**
Chairman and founder
Streetball Partners International

*E*very noble work is at first impossible.

—**THOMAS CARLYLE**

*T*o play
like a champion,
practice like a
champion.

—HJB

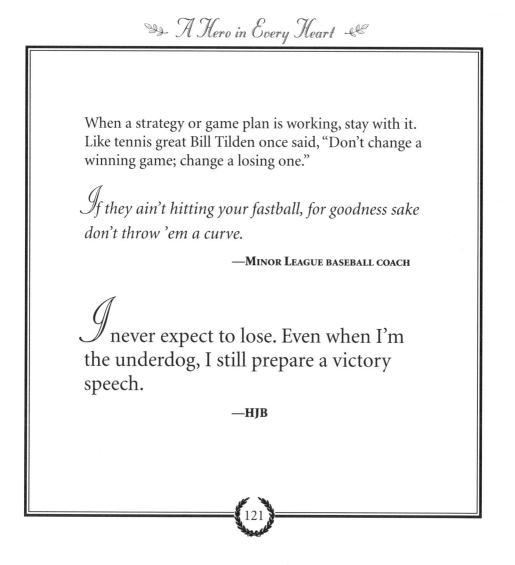

When a strategy or game plan is working, stay with it. Like tennis great Bill Tilden once said, "Don't change a winning game; change a losing one."

If they ain't hitting your fastball, for goodness sake don't throw 'em a curve.

—**MINOR LEAGUE BASEBALL COACH**

I never expect to lose. Even when I'm the underdog, I still prepare a victory speech.

—**HJB**

How we see ourselves is ultimately how others see us. Here's a story that will forever change the way you define the word disability.

My mission is to take the "dis" out of disability. What you have left is "ability." And that's what's important. My disability has enabled me to discover what my abilities really are. It's taught me a lot about character and determination.

I want my accomplishments to be examples to others that they, too, can accomplish whatever they set out to do.

Growing up for me was a challenge. When I was nine years old, my leg was amputated. I remember watching other kids go to school while I stood with my crutches and one leg.

But I got my life back. I went on to play base-ball, football, and hockey.

Today, as a Paralympian, I've won many gold and silver medals in national and international events. My message is that all of us are going to be faced with challenges—there's nothing we can do about that. How we prepare and how we decide to handle them is what makes the difference. God has made us in such a way that we can become victorious over the greatest odds.

—AL MEAD
Paralympian gold medalist,
Long Jump

*T*he road to success is a tollroad.

Winners commit themselves to constant self-improvement. Proper preparation always moves the dream closer.

I'm always training. Athletes are like a finely tuned car. You know the trouble you'd have if you let a Porsche or Ferrari sit in the garage.

—**Regina Jacobs**
Indoor World Championships
gold medalist, 1500-Meter

A winner is someone who talks himself out of his excuses.

—**Gin Miller**
Fitness expert

*N*othing
is more expensive
than a missed
opportunity.

—HJB

*N*ever let someone better you simply because he was better prepared.

—HJB

*E*verybody ought to do at least two things each day that he hates to do, just for practice.

—William James

*V*ictory belongs to the most persevering.

—Napoleon

Champions use adversity like a kite uses the wind; rising against it, they soar to new heights.

If others thought I couldn't do something because of my disability, I always figured out a way to do it. I was always in a tree or in the creek like any other kid. When I was still a little child I rode a skate- board with crutches held at my sides for balance. It freaked the neighbors, and they'd call my folks. They finally stopped calling and got used to me. I always challenged myself.

—**BRENDA LEVY**
Paralympic gold medalist,
Swimming

*N*othing is changed
by a mediocre
performance.

—HJB

*E*very athletic record achieved this year was once considered impossible.

*L*et us run with endurance the race that is set before us.

—**Hebrews 12:1**

*A*im high. That's where glory dwells.

—**HJB**

Victories that come as the result of fierce competition bring the most satisfaction.

The road to success is always under construction. You'll encounter potholes, detours, and delays. But you must keep your eye on your goal and keep moving forward.

—**ED TEMPLE**
Three-time Olympian, Coach
Track & Field

The only discipline that lasts is self-discipline.

—**B. PHILLIPS**

Never underestimate the power of dreams and the influence of the human spirit. We are all the same in this one notion: The potential for greatness lives within each of us.

My mother taught me very early to believe I could achieve any accomplishment I wanted to. The first was to walk without braces.

—WILMA RUDOLPH
*Four-time Olympic gold
medalist, Track & Field*

Where you find success, you find sacrifice.

—HJB

The Two Rules of Perseverance

Rule #1: Take one more step.

Rule #2: When you don't think you can take one more step, refer to rule #1.

—HJB

To be successful requires that we accept a certain amount of risk. We need to seek out tough and talented competition. This will test our courage, improve our strengths, and reveal our weaknesses.

Success is addictive. Once you feel the thrill of victory, you want to repeat it as often as possible. To be successful, you can't be afraid to take risks. Risk-taking means using your God-given abilities to overcome life's hurdles and sprint to the finish line.

—**BENITA FITZGERALD**
Olympic gold medalist,
100-Meter Hurdles

*C*ourage is grace under pressure.

—**ERNEST HEMINGWAY**

Heroes are important and necessary symbols of our hopes and dreams. But they aren't gods. They're flesh and blood like the rest of us. But when the test comes, heroes react in extraordinary ways. Rising above the ordinary, surpassing what would be expected, they never fail to inspire us to dream bigger, reach higher, and endure longer.

My mom and dad were heroes to me. Mom stressed the importance of treating all people equally. She taught me the importance of equal rights, and she blasted the hypocrisy of not accepting people because of the color of their skin. Mom backed up her words with actions.

Putting our heart and soul into something is a commitment we make to ourselves. It is our responsibility to do the best we can with what we have.

Another one of my heroes is Tom Landry. I could always trust him to do what he said he would do. He communicated his values by living them. He is a good man of great faith.

My wife and I have five children. To have their respect is the ultimate hall of fame. They see it all. They see how you treat each other. Getting and keeping their respect is what really matters. The question we must continually ask ourselves is, "How do we get to where we want to go and still remain a hero to those we love?"

—ROGER STAUBACH
Former Dallas Cowboys quarterback
Pro Football Hall of Fame

Champions have learned how to reach down deep for that extra reserve of spirit and pride.

My coach said, "Believe in yourself. Run with heart and put the rest aside." It's amazing how your body responds to your thoughts.

—**Carlette Guidry**
Olympian, 200-Meter
American women's record holder

*T*he importance of winning is not what we get from it, but what we become because of it.

—**HJB**

*E*very person needs
to have their moment in
the sun, when they raise
their arms in victory,
knowing that on this day,
at this hour, they were at
their very best.

—HJB

We're never too old to learn new skills and polish the ones we have. To grow in strength and to increase our speed and endurance is satisfying at any age.

I'm sixty-four now, and I did road running for five years strictly for health reasons. I was just a jogger until I learned about Masters Track & Field. My husband loved track-and-field, so we went out and tried it. I went in really not knowing what it was all about. I saw older women doing things women just don't do, like high jumping.

My greatest victory came in 1991 at the World Championship Masters in Finland. I set the world record in the heptathalon, which is seven events. I was in disbelief. I hadn't gone to the Masters with the goal of winning; I entered with the goal of doing better than my best.

My words of wisdom to young people go like this: If you're going to work at something, no matter if it's cleaning out a trash can or running a race, do a good job. I can't imagine doing anything and not doing my best.

—**BETTY VOSBURGH**
*Most Outstanding Female
Athlete in USA, 1991*

*I*f everyone who reached their full potential held a convention, they could all meet in the ballroom at the local Motel Six.

—**HJB**

All the acts of generosity and kindness that we extend to others eventually make a circle and come back to us. The Bible reminds us, "As we sow, so shall we reap."

Sports taught me about service. We are all servants. We're put on this earth to do the best we can and to help each other as we go along. And in turn we receive our rewards. The service I give to my family, to friends, to church, and to humankind is how I repay in some small way the many opportunities I was given when growing up.

I was known as the praying athlete. My mom always said, "If you take one step, God will take two." I used that, and I'd say, "Lord . . . here I go again!"

—**LUCINDA WILLIAMS ADAMS**
Olympic gold medalist,
Track & Field

Never miss an
opportunity to risk
being great.

—HJB

*A*s a coach I tell kids that whether you win or lose, act like a winner, and hold your head up high. Winning isn't everything, but trying to win is everything.

—**Pete Cava**
Coach, Media Consultant

*L*et perseverence be your engine and hope your fuel.

—**HJB**

*Y*ou build a successful life a day at a time.

—**Lou Holtz**

Wilma Rudolph overcame unimaginable odds to reach the 1960 Olympic games. As a young child she suffered from polio, scarlet fever, and other crippling diseases. She walked with a leg brace from the age of six until she was eleven. Hers is one of the most inspiring stories in the history of sports.

Wilma Rudolph was the most unusual athlete I've ever known. There was a magnetism and an aura about her. When she walked out on the track, she lit the place up. People in the stands went crazy. When the gun went off, she tiptoed down the track as if it belonged to her. It was something magnificent to see, and I can't say enough good things about her. She was so special.

—Marian Morgan
Former high school track coach

*I*f there are not great values behind great victories, the victories are pointless.

—**GREG SGROSSO**
High school basketball and tennis coach

*L*ife is tons of discipline.

—**ROBERT FROST**

*I*f a man does his best, what else is there?

—**GEORGE PATTON**

Average
is your enemy.

—PEARCE "ROCKY" LANE

We can ask for more opportunities or we can decide to make the most of those we already have. The latter course always produces results.

I was always told I couldn't do it. They told me that because we lived in the projects, I wasn't supposed to think about being a champion. Many people around me had a feeling of hopelessness. But I always felt like I was rich because my parents were there for me. My mother was a Girl Scout leader, and my father worked hard and was a dedicated parent. They taught me about hope. They said I could be anything I wanted to be if I wanted it bad enough. I believed them.

—**BARBARA JONES SLATER**
Olympic gold medalist,
Track & Field

146

*L*ast, but by no means least, courage—moral courage, the courage of one's convictions, the courage to see things through. The world is in a constant conspiracy against the brave. It's the age-old struggle—the roar of the crowd on one side and the voice of your conscience on the other.

—**Douglas MacArthur**

*E*very day, try to help someone who can't reciprocate your kindness.

—**Philosophy of**
Coach John Wooden

Every great achievement is the result of a heart on fire.

I'm very determined and stubborn. There's a desire in me that makes me want to do more and more, and to do it right.

Each of us has a fire in our heart for something. It's our goal in life to find it and to keep it lit.

—**MARY LOU RETTON**
Olympic gold medalist,
Gymnastics

*S*corn mediocrity. Embrace excellence.

—**HJB**

There lives
in each of us
a hero awaiting the
call to action.

—HJB

About the Authors

H. Jackson Brown Jr. is the author of fifteen books including the national best-sellers *Life's Little Instruction Book, P.S. I Love You,* and *Live and Learn and Pass It On.* His books have enjoyed worldwide acclaim and have been translated into more than twenty languages. He and his wife, Rosemary, live in Nashville.

Robyn Spizman is the author of numerous books including *The Thank You Book* and coauthor of *Good Behavior.* She has appeared for fifteen years as a consumer expert for NBC affilliate WXIA-TV's *Noonday.* She and her husband, Willy, and their two children, Justin and Ali, live in Atlanta.

Dear Reader,

If you have an inspiring story about a hero who's touched your life, we would love hearing from you. Our address is:

A Hero in Every Heart
P.O. Box 150285
Nashville, TN 37215